Filipiniana

PALMETTO
PUBLISHING
Charleston, SC
www.PalmettoPublishing.com

Hardcover ISBN: 979-8-8229-4032-1
Paperback ISBN: 979-8-8229-4312-4

Filipiniana

A COLLECTION OF PHILIPPINE POETRY IN ENGLISH

Marites V. Bundoc

To my beloved mother
Leticia,
whose faith in me
never wanes

Acknowledgments

I am grateful to my former professors, Professor Jessica Gilpatrick and Dr. Stavroula Kalogeras at Tiffin University, for their encouragement and belief that my capstone is publication-worthy.

To my family, especially my dear husband Mario, whose quiet but abiding support and endless patience have been extremely helpful in my finishing this project, and my daughter Kay, for her unflagging faith in me, my forever gratitude and love.

To all my relatives and friends for cheering me on, my sincere gratitude.

Lastly, I thank God for His constant guidance and provision.

Table of Contents

Introduction

I am now an American citizen and am grateful. I love my second home. However, I cannot shake off my Filipino heritage, for it flows in my veins. When I studied poetry writing last semester, I was inspired to write poetry with Philippine themes. That idea came to fruition in this capstone, where I wrote a collection of poems on the themes of Philippine myths, history, culture, landmarks, religion, and contemporary scenes.

The Filipinos are a poetic people. They see beauty in many things – in nature, music, poetry, dance, and the visual arts. However, while their Asian counterparts are well-represented in anthologies that serve as textbooks for literature studies, Filipino poets seem to have been forgotten. My studies in world literature recently have proven this assumption. In that class, we explored Chinese, Japanese, and Indian poetries but there was no entry from Philippine poetry. This motivated me even more to produce Philippine poetry in English. It may never be part of any anthology, but at least, I will have tried representing some aspects of Philippine history and culture, and hopefully revive a sense of Filipino identity and pride in the race into which I was born. This collection of poems is for anyone willing to listen, as poetry is supposed to be "spoken," or read orally, as in the days of the bards who handed down generations of oral tradition.

Incidentally, while doing research for this capstone, I found the book *Returning a Borrowed Tongue: An Anthology of Filipino and Filipino-American Poetry.* As its title suggests, this book, edited by Nick Carbo, is written by Filipino and Filipino-American poets. It is an anthology of contemporary Filipino poetry in English celebrating Filipino-American relations from the Second World War to the present (Carbo iv).

My collection of poems, on the other hand, is a modest attempt to depict Filipino history and culture from pre-Hispanic times to the present. It features the aboriginal, religious, social, and modern traditions. It talks about landmarks that make the Philippine geography part of the world's wonders. It celebrates the farmer, the fisherman, and the natives of the mountain provinces. It takes the reader back to ancient times when forests and hills were inhabited by fairies and other supernatural creatures. Before colonization, the natives of the Philippine islands believed in the spirits of the trees, the hills, the forests, and other natural things. They were pantheistic but religious, much like the ancient polytheistic Greeks. Then when the Borneans came to occupy Panay Island, the central region, some of the islanders imbibed the foreigners' Islamic faith, which traveled to the southern part of the Philippines, Mindanao, which remains a Muslim state to this day.

The Philippines was converted to Catholicism during the Spanish colonization and remains predominantly Catholic, although there are other Protestant denominations and reborn Christians there today as well. The Philippines has gone through two world wars, Spanish and Japanese subjugations, and calamities like tsunamis and volcanic eruptions. Yet, their faith in a supreme Being, whose works they have seen in beautiful and bountiful nature the country endowed with, has never waned. This is the single most important source of their strength that has made them rise time and again after each fall.

My poetry collection likewise describes the history of the islands and their people and depicts the pastoral life of rural communities. "The Barter of Panaii" and "Life in the Village" are among those poems. It also showcases some contemporary scenes, with signs of modernization everywhere, and what it means to live in The Philippines today. "The Philippines Old and New" features those scenes.

The most nostalgic part of Philippine history, however, was the period of colonization under Spain from the sixteenth to the nineteenth centuries, when many Filipinos died in the uprising against the oppressive practices of the Spaniards in The Philippines. Heroes like Apolinario Mabini, Emilio Aguinaldo, and Manuel Quezon led the Filipinos in their revolt against the "Mother" country (Ileto 67). Most notable of all, although he was never part of a bloody revolution, was Jose Rizal (77), a Filipino ophthalmologist educated in Europe. Rizal wrote two novels in Spanish, *Noli Me Tangere* (*The Social Cancer*) and *El Filibusterismo* (*The Reign of Greed*), which stirred patriotism among the Filipinos (78), as his novels exposed the brutalities and exploitation of the natives by the Spaniards. Upon returning to Manila from Europe, Rizal was arrested, imprisoned, and executed but became the Philippine national hero (78). His monument stands in the now Rizal Park in Manila as a testament to the heroic offering of his life for the freedom of his beloved country.

Filipino poetry in English dates back to 1905 when it first appeared in *The Filipino Students' Magazine* in Berkeley, California (Carbo iv). Since it is contemporary, the poems in the anthology that Carbo edited are written in free verse, which seems to portray The Philippines emerging as a liberated nation, no longer under any foreign rule.

In contrast, my collection represents the Filipino spirit from its beginnings to the present. Hence, I wrote in ballads, odes, elegies, sonnets, sestinas, villanelles, rubais, and other prosodic forms, including a comic limerick, which I have entitled "Good Old Father P" – forms which I learned in my Poetry Writing course I also wrote poems following the conventions of exotic forms like the Filipino Tanaka, the Chinese Haiku, and the Japanese tanka or waka. My studies in American Literature have also encouraged me to experiment with free verse, somehow in the styles of Walt Whitman and Emily Dickinson.

Philippine heritage is rich in history and culture, predating Spanish colonization in the sixteenth century. The poems in this collection trace the history of the Filipino people, especially of the Visayans of central Philippines, where I hail from, from a barter that, according to legend, occurred between ten Bornean *datus*, or chieftains, who were fleeing from their tyrannical king. Sailing aboard their *binidays*, boats shaped like a canoe, they left Borneo with their wives and treasures and landed on the shores of Panaii (originally spelled *Panay*, but for the sake of phonology in the poem, I adopted the spelling "Panaii"). The *datus* of Malay origins were royalty back in their country and their faith was Islamic. They bargained with the ruler of *Panay*, King

Marikudo, to trade his island for a golden *salakot* ("hat)," a strand of gold necklace for his wife Queen Maniwangtiwan, and an array of trinkets. The barter was done, and the natives retreated to the mountains while the Borneans settled in the lowlands. Thus, aborigines called "Agtas," could be seen in the mountain provinces in the Philippines, who, due to their nomadic culture and hunting ways, are struggling to survive as they are hardly able to adapt to the rapidly changing industrial times (Headland). They are small people with very dark skins and curly hair, and they live on hunting in the forests. The Malays, on the other hand, are of the brown race; that is why Filipinos are brown. They descend from the Bornean-Malayan stock. "Legend of the Barter of Panaii" tries to capture this ancient tale.

The Philippines was "discovered" in 1521 by Ferdinand Magellan, a Portuguese explorer working for King Phillip the Second of Spain (California State University Bakersfield). Spanish explorer Ruy Lopez de Villalobos named the archipelago *Las Islas Filipinas* ("The Philippine Islands") in honor of the Spanish monarch in 1543 (Embassy of the Philippines Madrid, Spain). The Spanish *conquistadores* ("conquerors") called the country – which was not a country then but a group of city-states each ruled by its own chieftain, like those of ancient Greece –" islas" because The Philippines is a land made up of many islands. Again, geographically, it had a similarity with the Greek islands. A main feature of the country, therefore, was the sea, and many Filipinos were and are seafaring to this day. I also tried to capture this feature of Philippine life in "Reflections of a Seaman," influenced by *The Odyssey* (Homer 277), and "A Seaman's Soliloquy."

For almost four centuries, The Philippines was a colony of Spain, during which the Filipinos suffered untold misery and servitude in a land which, by right of birth was theirs. Robert Frost's poetry, which often mentions sap, resin, or other fluids from "bleeding trees" (Sholes), can be interpreted as metaphorical about the suffering of people under foreign domination. The Philippines struggled for independence during the last years of Spanish oppression leading to the Philippine Revolution of 1898 and against Japanese invaders until Japan surrendered to General Douglas MacArthur on board the USS Missouri in Tokyo Bay on September 6, 1945 (National Archives), which ended the war in the Pacific and freed The Philippines. Frost's "The Road Not Taken" has often inspired me to choose "the one less traveled by" (Frost qt. in Levine 253 19) as those Filipinos did to regain the country's freedom. I hope that my humble poetry can shed a ray of light to aid the modern Filipino struggling against the oppression of poverty and political corruption. Sometimes, we need to look back to the sacrifices of our forebears to recognize our intrinsic rights as a people – free under God, before whom all men are equal. "Attack of the Capital" and "The Liberation of Panaii describe those momentous events in history, the Second World War and the Filipino-Japanese War.

One of the poets who stood out in my world literature course was the Chinese Du Fu, a poet-historian of Song Dynasty China (Puchner et al. 1316). Du Fu rose to canonical Chinese literature because of his ability to capture the dramatic historical events and spirit of his age (1316). He understood that the An Lushan Uprising was a significant historical event poetically, but the depth of his voice came from his ability to convey how the rebellion affected his life and the lives of the people around him (1316). He has influenced my creative work because, in his poems, he painted similar pictures of life among the Filipinos who fought during the Spanish Revolution of 1898, the Filipino-Japanese War of the 1940s, and the devastation that resulted from those upheavals (1316). In "Spring Prospects," he wrote of the old people waiting for their sons to come home from the war, many of whom never returned:

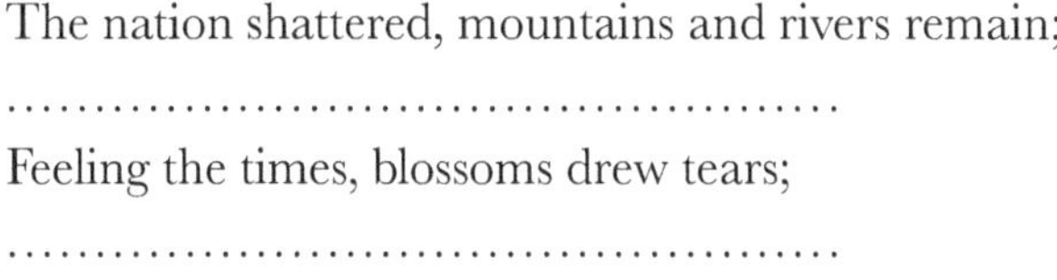

> The nation shattered, mountains and rivers remain;
>
> . . . .
>
> Feeling the times, blossoms drew tears;
>
> . . . .
>
> A letter from home worth ten thousand in gold.
>
> White hairs, fewer for the scratching. (Du qtd. in Puchner et al. 1317 1, 3, 6-7)

The poverty in early China after the An Lushan Revolution was paralleled by the poor people's plight in the post-war Philippines, as seen in these lines from Du Fu's poem "My Thatched Roof Is Ruined by the Autumn Wind:"

> Above the bed, the roof leaked,
>
> No place was dry,
>
> And the raindrops ran down like strings, without a break. (Du qtd. in Puchner et al. 1318)

My goal for this project is to give the Filipino a chance to revisit his past and rediscover his unique identity, through the beautiful genre of poetry, which is in keeping with the Filipino heritage. Today, the Tagalogs still stage the traditional "Balagtasan," "a poetic joust after the *duplo* of the nineteenth century," and it was attributed to Francisco Baltazar as Balagtas, a Filipino poet during the Spanish times (Almario). This idea was also inspired by my studies of Taiwanese literature, whereby the Taiwanese people have endeavored during the past century to establish their national identity after having been colonized by the Dutch, Spaniards, Japanese, and even, arguably, the Americans (Jacobs). Moreover, I was influenced by the Irish writer James Joyce who left Ireland and moved to France but whose writings were always about Ireland (Puchner 1168), generally, and Dublin, specifically (Damrosch and Dettmar 2215). "The Angelus" was inspired by Joyce's "From Ulysses" (2267).

Some of Longfellow's verses in "A Psalm for Life" sound like they are addressed to the Filipinos during colonial times as well as modern Filipinos who might have forgotten their legacy and have become complacent. They also describe the Philippine National hero Jose Rizal and the heroes who fought hard with their lives to gain the country's independence:

Lives of great men all remind us

We can make our lives sublime,

And, departing, leave behind us

Footprints on the sands of time. (Longfellow qtd. in Poetry Foundation)

The Filipinos have risen, time and again, Phoenix-like, from every adversity brought about by colonization, foreign subjugation, enculturation, and indoctrination, and have proven themselves as worthy citizens of a free world. The Philippines has produced men of letters including the multi-awarded Jose Garcia Villa, who received a Poetry Award from the American Academy of Poets, Academy of Arts and Letters, a Rockefeller Foundation Award, and a Shelley Memorial Award. He studied at the University of New Mexico and later moved to New York where he lived, taught, and died at the age of eighty-eight (Academy of American Poets). I also wrote nationalistic poems to celebrate the resilience of the Filipino spirit in the face of all odds. "Arise and Shine" is about honoring the legacy of our forebears and carrying on the torch of freedom.

I have grouped the poems in this collection by themes. First is Philippine history and legends, folklore, and superstitious beliefs before the arrival of the Spaniards." "Beliefs in Unseen Beings," "The Legend of the Filipino Witch," and "Aboriginal Beliefs" depict those ancient Philippine myths.

The next set of poems portrays the colonial times under the Spaniards who introduced Catholicism to the natives. Religious and social traditional celebrations follow. The Filipinos are religious by culture, as they were taught by Spanish missionaries. Comparable to their unquestioning faith in God's will is Anne Bradstreet's Puritan faith expressed in her poetry. Taking care of a household with eight children during the early colonization days in the seventeenth century, with her husband always away at work, braving a physical condition that always had her bedridden, and still being able to write the first American poems written by a woman, was nothing short of admirable (Levine et al. 115 - 22). Her challenges, made surmountable by her unwavering faith in a providing God, and her spirit of wonder at the works of God (Bradstreet 115), are relatable to Filipino mothers, many of whom are poor economically but rich spiritually. "Passion Play" is a poem that reflects the Filipino faith in a redeeming God and "The Harvest" celebrates their thanksgiving to the God who provides.

William Butler Yeats' poem "The Lake of Isle Innisfree" has inspired my poems related to nature – the mountains, the rice terraces, the seas, and pastoral scenes, such as harvest time celebrations. As Yeats went back to Ireland to his mother's native town of Sligo, he was inspired by the beauty of the countryside in a way that London never had (Damrosch and Dettmar 2174). His lines remind me of the beautiful countryside in my mother's hometown:

I will arise and go now, and go to Innisfree,

....

And I shall have some peace there, for ...peace comes dropping slow,
Dropping from the veils of the morning
to where the crickets sing.

(Yeats qtd. in Damrosch and Dettmar 2174 1, 5-6). In my poetry, I am also revisiting my ancestors' rural town of Barotac Nuevo in the Philippines, particularly the river by my grandmother's farm where I used to play rafting with my cousin during our summer breaks. "The Gentle Rivulet" was inspired by Yeats' poem.

I have always been an admirer of the British poet William Wordsworth, who was not only a Romanticist but also a nationalist. He wrote poems about the beauty of his parents' rural Lake District in England and also of freedom, as in the seventeenth poem in "Poems of National Independence and Liberty:"

When lawless violence

Invades a Realm, so pressed that in the scale

Of perilous war, her weightiest armies fail,

Honour is hopeful elevation – whence

Glory, and triumph. (Wordsworth 1377)

Reading these verses, the Filipino under subjugation to foreign rule might ask, "How did the poet know about my plight?" That is because the desire for independence is a universal sentiment. England had colonies in the East, too, but after the Second World War, its East Asian and Southeast Asian colonies were occupied by Japan (British Empire, Co.). My poems "The Countryside" and "Arise and Shine" have bearings of Wordsworth's influence.

I have dedicated a section of my collection to the Philippine national hero Jose Rizal, who has always been one of my models of nationalism and patriotism. The American Revolution of 1776 and the French Revolution of 1789 were two significant political upheavals that resulted from the Enlightenment practice of changing authority (Stevens 108). The American struggle to break free from colonial Great Britain was similar to the Philippine struggle for independence from Spain, with the difference that it took almost four centuries for the Filipinos to realize their goal. These revolutions grew out of revolutionary political writings, especially the ideas of Voltaire, Locke, and Rosseau during the Age of Enlightenment, from the mid-seventeenth to the end of the eighteenth century (Stevens 97). In his writings, Rosseau argues that all men are born free and are entitled to life, liberty, and property (108). Locke in his turn holds that it is the people's will that gives governments their authority (108). Similarly, Rosseau claims in the opening of his 1762 book *The Social Contract* that although man was born free, he was constantly under servitude (Stevens 108). According to Rosseau, free people engage in a "social contract" for the common good, and governments that fail to look after the interests of their citizens are legitimately dissolvable (108). Philippine national hero Jose Rizal was educated in Europe and was an intellectual, a philologist, an ophthalmologist, a polyglot, an author, and a poet (de Ocampo). Yeats' "Easter 1916" talks of the common Irish man and woman who participated in the uprising against England until the Irish Republic was declared on Easter Monday, April 24, 1916 (Damrosch and Dettmar 2181). Similarly, the Filipinos rose in revolt against Spain which ended in Spain's secession of the Philippines to the United States for twenty million dollars at the Treaty of Paris in 1898 (Harvard). Then in the Second World War, the Philippines and the United States fought against Japan after which the Philippines gained its independence from the United States and became officially a Republic on July 4, 1946 (National Archives).

One of the significant ideologies of the nineteenth century was nationalism. People started to perceive themselves as citizens of a country bound together by a common language, cultural or literary tradition, or even a shared racial or ethnic heritage rather than as citizens of little principalities or vast empires (Stevens 129). Similar to national flags, national anthems, and national sports teams, literary traditions can serve the same purpose of bringing a group of people together (129). Rizal's novels served this purpose as well. His works awakened the consciousness of the Filipino people who began to form associations promoting unity among the various regions in the Philippines (Ileto 77). "Philippine Symbols" is about the national emblems of The Philippines, which signify to Filipinos their new-found independence, sovereignty, and uniqueness as a nation.

Tagalog was chosen as the foundation for the adoption of the Philippine national language, according to a proclamation made by Manuel L. Quezon, president of the Commonwealth Republic, on December 30, 1937 (Savella). Following the EDSA Revolution in 1986, the Philippine Constitution declared Tagalog-based Filipino as the official language (Savella). The official languages of the Philippines today are Filipino and English. Thus, terms like "bathala," ("God") and "Banaue" ("Mountain Province") are incorporated into this collection of Philippine poetry in English. A footnote is included to furnish the reader with an English translation where needed.

Yeats witnessed the chaotic times of the Irish resistance movements against British rule in Northern Ireland (Damrosch and Dettmar 2183). It was at this concerning time that his daughter Anne was born. While his poem "A Prayer for My Daughter" talks about the poet's worries about the future of his child in a world that is slowly decaying in the face of political upheavals, it likewise articulates a nationalistic concern for the future of the Irish. This is a theme that also pervades Philippine literature in English. The 1970s, era of the late President Marcos, was likewise a time of political chaos and civil unrest which led to the People's Revolution, also known as the EDSA, on February 22-25, 1986 (Sanchez). This tumult ousted President Marcos from the country and exiled him to Hawaii with his family. The Filipinos were uneasy during those times; they feared for their children and their future. For many, Imelda Marcos, in her blind imitation of Argentina's Evita Peron, was partly instrumental to the fatality of Marcos' governance. Yeats' poetry is, thus, informative and influential in the writing of my poetry on nationalism and civil liberty. "A Hero's Vow" and "A Nation Lost" are among those poems.

My studies in nineteenth-century American Literature featured antislavery poems and essays. Henry Wadsworth Longfellow's poem "The Slave Singing at Midnight" particularly left an imprint on me and influenced my poetry about the slavery that the Filipinos were subjected to during the Spanish colonization:

Loud he sang the psalm of David!

He, a Negro and enslaved,

Sang of Israel's victory,

Sang of Zion, bright and free. (Longfellow qtd. in Levine et al. 710)

His book *Poems on Slavery* helped me imagine the horrors of colonial bondage. In his verses, Longfellow highlights his faith in Jesus as the Redeemer of men and the liberator of the slave. He alludes to the Bible in the *Psalms* and warns the oppressor that this commonwealth may crumble in the weight of its mechanism of slavery, even as Samson brought down the pillars of the palace, and in the gospel where Paul and Silas are in prison and their singing of hymns to God broke their chains and freed them. Throughout this book, Longfellow talks about God and his compassion for the captives.

Indeed, there was a similarity between African slavery in America and Filipino slavery under the Spanish colonizers. Longfellow's *Poems* likewise express adherence to the principles embodied in the scriptures. "The Good Part That Shall Not Be Taken Away" is an allusion to Jesus' admonition to Martha, Mary's sister who complains that Mary is not helping her prepare a meal for Jesus; instead, she is by Jesus' feet and is listening to him speak. Jesus tells her that Mary has chosen the better part and it shall not be taken away from her (*Power for Life Bible*, Lk. 10.38-41). This poem also influenced my poetry on liberation. The main character in this poem is a schoolteacher, probably a Christian missionary, who talks to the native Indian children in the village school of the "Great Kenhawa" about Jesus, the Messiah who sets the captives free:

She reads them at eventide
Of One who came to save;
To cast the captive's chain aside
And liberate the slave. (Longfellow 7)

I could only imagine how the Filipinos, who were called *Indios* (a name which means inferior, good-for-nothing, indolent), by the Spanish colonizers, felt each time they were made to bow every time they met a Spanish priest and kiss their hand lest they be slapped for disrespect. I could also imagine how the Filipino servants in the Spanish households were treated like low-class citizens, unable to join them at the dinner table, always relegated to the background except when they were serving their masters. As in the slavery tales of American authors (Levine 815-1066), I believe that many Filipino women were abused by their masters and suffered humiliation and degradation. During the Japanese occupation, they also underwent unthinkable suffering – particularly the women who were enslaved for Japanese men's sensual pleasure. It is, indeed, sad to think back to those moments in Philippine history, but they need to be recapitulated and exposed for the world to know. One cannot sugar-coat the lessons of history.

Like that schoolteacher in the American colonies, Christian missionaries came to the Philippine shores in the sixteenth century onward and taught the villagers about Jesus, how to read the Bible, and how to pray the "Lord's Prayer" and other prayers. They introduced church hymns, some of them in Latin, which I sang in the parish choir even though I did not understand them. "May Flower Devotion" features the children's veneration of the Virgin Mary as they offer flowers and songs to her in the month of May when schools are closed for the summer break. The faith and religiosity of the Filipino people are reflected in such poems as "Ode to the Virgin Mary" and "The Fiesta." Feast days in honor of saints, the passion play during the Lenten season, and the celebration of Easter and Christmas also depict the Filipinos' devotion to God and veneration of the saints. Tagore's *Gitanjali* ("Song Offerings"), a collection of poems expressing his devotion to God has been influential in this part of my collection as well.

Today the summer has come at my window with its sighs and murmurs; and the bees

Are playing their minstrelsy at the court of the flowering grove.

Now it is time to sit quiet, face to faith with thee, and to sing dedication of life in this silent and overflowing leisure. (Tagore 5)

Philippine poetry is also influenced by the Romantic Movement of the nineteenth century. While the Romanticists did not want to go back to the Medieval Age, poets like William Wordsworth and Percy Bysshe Shelley looked back with nostalgia to the past where nature was a source of inspiration (Stevens 125). Wordsworth wrote "Tintern Abbey" after his walk with his sister Dorothy on the Welsh Borders:

Therefore I am still

A lover of the meadows and the woods,

And mountains; and of all that we behold

From this green earth. (qtd. in Damrosch and Dettmar 431 429 - 433)

Conversely, Shelley expressed his love of nature in "Mont Blanc: *Lines Written in the Vale of Chamouni*" –

In the wild woods, among the mountains lone,

Where waterfalls around it leap forever,

Where woods and winds contend, and a vast river

Over its rocks ceaselessly bursts and raves. (qtd. in Damrosch and Dettmar 871-5) "Mount Madjaas," "Mount Mayon," and "Aurora, the Philippines' Hidden Paradise," are some of my poems that talk about the grandeur and beauty of nature. The last of the three aforementioned poems is especially a plea to preserve wildlife and the culture of the aboriginal tribes.

To the Romanticists, specifically Samuel Taylor Coleridge, the use of the imagination was paramount; he argued for the "willing suspension of disbelief" called "poetic faith," whereby he asks readers of fiction to accept the possibility of supernatural events (Stevens 124). It is a Romanticist notion since the object of an artistic work is the elevation of the soul, what Poe calls the "poetic sentiment," not to teach a lesson (Levine 653-4). Belief in the supernatural was also present in his works, such as in Coleridge's poem "The Rime of Ancient Mariner." The Romantic Gothic genre is popular in the Philippines and can be seen in many artistic works such as stories, movies, visuals, and other graphic works of art. "Belief in Unseen Beings" captures the theme of belief in witches, fairies, and other supernatural beings among early Filipinos.

I also wrote poems about Iloilo City and the island of Panay where I came from. Panay is located in the Visayan Region, the central part of the Philippines. The only novel in English written by a Visayan is *Without Seeing the Dawn* by Esteban Javellana. This novel, which I studied in my undergraduate major in Comparative Literature, is about the Japanese cruelties in the Panay Province during the Japanese Occupation in the early 1940s. I hope my simple poetry can somehow add to Visayan literature in English. In this collection, I feature traditional celebrations like the "Dinagyang," the yearly Mardi Gras in honor of the Holy Child Jesus on his presentation to the Magi from the east, popularly known as the Three Kings. This event also celebrates the "Ati" (aborigines of Panay) tribes; that is why the participants paint themselves to look like the ancestral people of the island and don costumes and artificial armor of the hunting tribes.

The last part of my poetry collection is about the current scenario in the Philippine socio-economic landscape, where the gap between the rich and the poor is widening more than ever. According to World Bank, the middle class in the Philippines had expanded to nearly twelve million people and the economically secure population had risen to forty-four million in 2018 (World Bank). However, inequality is still very high: the richest one percent of earners collectively receive seventeen percent of the nation's income, while the lowest fifty percent receive only fourteen percent. Despite being one of the economies in the area with the greatest growth, USAID says that "many Filipinos are left behind" (USAID). This reminds one of the oppressive Spanish *encomienda* system, a fiefdom where the natives were made to rent their own land then in the hands of the Spanish landlords and pay taxes to the landlords come harvesttime. Or, worse, the landlords took the harvest and gave only a small portion of it to the tenant.

Children of the rich go to expensive schools – as in the convent school system of the Spanish times – while the poorer families cannot afford to send their children to college as the cost of tertiary education in the Philippines has gone up tremendously. Poorer children are at a disadvantage because, due to their socioeconomic status, they either start school late or drop out because they need to help in their households (Department of Education). In rural areas, poor road conditions affect teachers, who come to school only three times a week; educational materials are delayed or never delivered (Department of Education). Data from the local survey and national government statistics show that the "goal of education for all" has not been reached (Department of Education).

According to the government's midterm progress report on the eight Millennium Development Goals (MDGs), Goal No. 2 on universal primary education and Goal No. 5 on maternal health are the two that are currently facing the greatest threats (Macasero). The Department of Education reports that the country currently lacks 159,000 classrooms for the 2023– 2024 school year. This is a more serious shortfall than the 91,000-classroom deficit from the previous year (Macasero). "Philippines Old and New" captures this ironic contrast – a mixture of the grand old classic architecture and rich mansions on the one hand and the impoverished slum areas on the other hand.

A significant feature of modern life in the Philippines is immigration, whereby Filipinos emigrate to the United States and adopt it as their second home. This trend is not new, however.

Escaping enslavement and forced labor in the Spanish Galleon trade, Filipinos began migrating to the United States in the seventeenth century, establishing their first settlement in St. Malo, Louisiana, and through the next centuries, other Filipino groups, such as mariners, domestics, and adventurers, came and spread all over the country

(Stanford University). As of 2021, there were nearly two million Filipinos living in the United States (Davis and Batalova), helping to boost the American economy as well as remitting money to their homeland. Filipino Americans are among the largest dollar contributors to the Philippine economy, with remittances having risen to $38 billion as of 2022 (Davis and Batalova). America has given many Filipinos a safe haven as they leave their native land in search of a better life and better opportunities both for themselves and their families, as most of them, when they become American citizens, petition their relatives to come as well. This is by far one of the largest diasporas in history. However, it is a phenomenon that is not unique to Filipinos. Other nationalities, like the Chinese, Indians, and Japanese have done the same. As of 2019, the estimated number of Asian immigrants in the United States rose to 22.4 million, comprising about seven percent of the nation's population (Budiman and Ruiz).

Filipino poetry in English has come a long way. Since English is the second official language in the Philippines today, I believe there are more Filipino and Filipino-American poets out there who are writing in English about their homeland but are not recognized, and one of the reasons for that neglect is likely due to a lack of resources. My wish, therefore, is for Filipino writers in English to be given opportunities to hone their skills and contribute to the rich heritage that is Philippine poetry. The Philippines is a great country and Philippine literature is a rich field waiting to be cultivated.

Invocation to the Muse

O Muse of Poetry, do come to me.
O show thy words, alliterating rhymes.
That as, on strings of lute, my poems be
a chord of melody that sways with chimes.

Belief in Unseen Beings

Once far away on islands fair, the natives had
a god with powers high above all gods.
He kept them from becoming truly bad,
protected them from nature's rushing floods.
Bathala[1] was his name; he was adored.
Libations poured, worshipful dances mixed
with songs and prayers to their Lord
amidst their lances and their wives betwixt.

But there were lesser gods for some as well -
the spirits of their dead – of Chinese lore –
they worshipped all – they rang the tiny bell
to signal the spirit's presence and adore.
The trees had spirits, too, or so they thought.
And so they never harmed them; they were trees
whose leaves and branches coolness, comfort, brought
to mankind; nests for birds and hives for bees.

---

[1] *Bathala* is the Filipino word for a Supreme Being (God)

Legend of the Filipino Evil Witch

Legend says that evil lurked in forests
deep - witches on the watch when
people were asleep. Dark and devious
spirits they assumed female beauty
but men's blood consumed.

 Man, beware, the beauty by your
side, you conceive to be your
faultless little bride, heiress to
Medusa, serpentine,
waits for darkness, says, "You're mine!"

Aboriginal Beliefs

In ancient times our ancestors believed
That spirits lived in trees, and no one dared
trespass the bounty Nature had conceived
To pause and ponder - question no one cared.

The hills and dales, too, were inhabited
by fairies beautiful with flowing hairs.
To cross their dwellings was prohibited
so children needed not to shed their tears.

In forests, there were giants and ogres.
They're harmless left alone; when challenged, though,
they'll throw a rock on you, beware, tricksters,
as Cyclops did on proud Odysseus' bow.

The sea that deeply teemed with creatures strange
would lure our mariners onboard their ship.
True figures with some tricks their forms could
change if trusting men to water they would dip.

But most of that did change when Spaniards came.
They taught our folks the meaning of the cross –
that their souls purified no more to blame
for Christ assumed man's sure eternal loss.

Fort Santiago

Through centuries your walls are standing still -
rock of defense against the enemy.
A mark of nation's might and staunchest will,
a memory of sixteenth century.

Rock of defense against the enemy,
In fifteen sev'nty-one, the Spanish built
a memory of sixteenth century.
They fortified you to the hilt.

In fifteen sev'nty-one, the Spanish built
to honor Jesus' brother, his name, James.
The Spanish fortified you to the hilt -
formidable, endowed with lofty aims.

To honor Jesus' brother, his name James,
they named you after him – Santiago –
formidable with lofty aims.
Did they adorn you with the Virgin's grotto?

They named you after him – Santiago –
Did they adorn you with the Virgin's grotto?
Your walls protected our valiant heroes.
On your walls are inscribed our heroes' woes.

On your walls are inscribed our heroes' woes -
be Spanish, Japanese, American.
Your walls protected our valiant heroes,
your strength enforced by Holy Vatican.

The Filipino flag you proudly bear –
the symbol of our nation's might and will.
Mark of our freedom you're forever there;
through centuries your walls are standing still!

Ode to the Blessed Virgin

O you who prophesied that blessed you would be called
through all the generations of the men
and women of the world, this faith of old.

You cried oe'r the sad story of man's case
so you bore heaven's Prince of mercy and
undying love; bear us to your Son's grace.

A country's people venerate you still.
They call you "Mother," "Virgin," able help.
Do bend to Jesus' love the faithful's will.

Your grotto stands on islands near and far
across the land where everyone beholds
such loveliness; no vision ever mar.

Inspire our youth with spirits of sublime
nobility, harmonious love for men.
Divine Love may they realize in time.

Your pleas, your supplications, Jesus hears
as in the wedded couple's need for wine.
To heaven's ears our pray'rs with love He bears.

The *Fiesta* (Feast)

The church bells ring this early morn.
I hear the music through the walls
from young lad practicing his horn.

"It's fiesta time! Come one and all!
Don your best garbs; wear your smiles.
Let's to the feast our neighbors call!"

The men take out their roasting poles;
the womenfolk their aprons on,
that later fires produce on coals.

All kinds of fragrant fruits are on
the tables long adorned with flow'rs
the maidens brought at crack of dawn.

"Here comes the band – the trumpets, horns,
the cymbals, and the xylophones.
They signal one of cheerful morns.

Let's celebrate the birth of one
who by her "yes," the Prince of Light
against the dark forever won!

The *Angelus* (Vespers)

Twilight comes, steeple bells are rung.
People pause; the "Angelus" is sung,
"Behold the lowly handmaid of the Lord.
My humble will be bent to your accord."

Tradition comes but once in hundred years –
the Spanish missions brought with cross and cheers.
For Mary's Annunciation brought the world
its Savior, pure, and lovely to behold.

The Barter of Panaii

Ten chieftains from the land of Borneo
sailed on the South Seas, reached our shores.
The natives led by King Marikudo
For long years peaceful, never went to wars.

The chieftains asked for land by sweet exchange
of golden hat, some trinkets, gold, as gain,
and shining chain for beauteous Queen - though strange.
"If yes, on yonder mountains please remain."

And that was how Panaii was sold to them
Who fled a tyrant king back on their land.
They found this new land such a sparkling gem -
a free home for them and their avid band.

The friendly natives promptly made retreat
to yonder mountains up above the plains.
"We will be friends forever, we entreat.
Respect our wills to hold our mutual gains."

Bornean Malay race since then we bore –
the blood of royals coursing through our veins.
A glorious race dwelt on our shores before
the Spaniards came and tied us to the chains.

Attack of the Capital

For now you thought the world asleep
a dragon to its lair has lured you in.
For though today it's crumbled in the dust,
same nation that you crushed will be the one
to have you stung and hurled around upturned,
and guess whose turn in agony is next!

A serpent bruised will bite the heel – yours next.
While seeming gone, it's really not asleep!
That which you defeated, they're within
 their mighty Council; soon you'll turn to dust.
At end of day, for sure there's only one –
victorious flag – their honor, pride returned.

So then, their glorious liberty returned
delivered by MacArthur in the next
four years. Now no one truly was asleep
till Umezo's signed names complete were in.
From Filipinos' boots wipe off the dust;
America, at last, victorious one!

O glorious one, the battle is upturned.
What are you questing next? Stay not asleep.
Your heroes' woes in mind turn not to dust.

A Hero's Vow

God gave this land for me to have and hold,
a land where children could be free and bold
but now in Spanish servitude to be
enslaved in shame; I am no longer free.

And thus began my awful tragic tale – my
people lived in fearful, mournful vale.
We toiled, obeyed, and knelt in silent pain,
asked why this heavy burden on us lain.

A vast empire, it should contented be.
Yet it impinged on people's liberty.
With cross and arms, they conquered all the land
and planted Philip's flag on our white sand.

But now, O Lion, mighty, greedy, I
shall rise on Eagle's wings though now I die.
To foreign pow'r our children shall not bow.
They will be free at last; this is my vow!

The Slave

When to abject oppression I succumb,
my soul is crushed, my heart is pricked to bleed.
My body weak, my head spins; I feel numb.
I ask why man is wont to such a deed.

Forefathers free, this land of liberty -
colonials came and took my land from me
They robbed and stripped me of my dignity;
they called me, "slave," displayed for all to see.

To endless toil, I am a subject-bound
to unjust serfdom, bondage as of old
when Israel by cruel Pharaoh found
obedient builders – monuments, behold!

God's promise: the enslaved set free - I claim
His pledge. I, heaven's mercy thus proclaim.

"Pearl of Orient Seas"

O nation great, o land of setting sun,
for you our martyrs died for you're but one.
For you, our heroes braved the painful fight
with "Mother" Spain, the Lion, in its might.

Arise today, o noble men, we pray.
Uphold our land that precious honor may
 deserve the glory of our dignity;
'twas forged on blood to win our destiny.

Today, do you succumb to fear or greed
to feed some wily, grievous, misplaced need?
O would that you do not forget the deeds
of martyrs brave who died for our blessed needs!

Pearl of the Orient Seas, behold your face –
on broken mirrors shaming heroes' grace!
Awake and hear our people's silent cries;
o raise our flag, pray not one hither dies.

Liberation of Panaii

In silence, soldiers crept along the shore
of island's coconut-lined beaches, in
Panaii's exotic lands and mountains deep.
The Japanese did not expect that soon,
 the force of US fleets will corner them
 and force them to surrender at long last.

This happened fast with little casualty
with help from Filipinos' underground
civilian militants. The native folks
 rejoiced with glee at MacArthur's return.
At last, they claimed their province free once more!

"Hurrah, hurrah, to freedom we all march!
Adorn the streets! Take out your trumpets and
French horns. Glad tidings, friends, from USA
brought to our shores. Today, from Japs we're free!

The Gentle Rivulet

The rays of golden sun upon the stalks of rice
on grandma's farm as soon as I arise,
the gentle rivulet beckons me - "Come
and play this day with me in glee and calm."

The chirping chickadee by riverbed –
away it flies; here comes a parrot in its stead.
The gentle rivulet and child's imaginings –
a love for poetry in its beginnings.

The Countryside

I walk along the beach and find
a charm so willful and so free.
The country's beauty blows my mind!

The trees of coconut and palms
line up the shores of sparkling sand.
They say, "We're held by God's strong arms!"

The jasmines on the way, the buds
of lilacs, too, breathe scents of peace.
No wonder locals beat the odds!

Then fragrance that was – oh, divine,
so filled the air with sweet caress!
The pork man's roast to taste incline.

The locals live a simple life.
Yet happily they do surprise.
A peaceful life – they have no strife.

Exotic plants I've never seen,
a perfect cone, those choc'late hills,
and forests' verdant mountains green.

The rapid falls cascading fast
provide great power to the plains.
These falls are found on mountains vast.

The countryside provides a home
to many local folks beneath
the mountains under blue sky's dome.

The lowly chickadee, now free,
where once encaged in bitter misery,
can now roam free where'er it wants to be!

I thank the Lord for countryside.
Its spirit gave my soul a lift
that summer when I walked aside.

Mount Madjaas

Northeast of Borneo the Muja Island state -
an island in the Philippines called Mayd
Madj(a) es - Panaii - subdued by Chola state
Panaiinons lived inside Sumatra's gate,
refusing Taoist, Hindu, Muslim faith.
Hail, Mount Madjaas, grand, majestic,
standing tall and mighty as an emblem.
Your children sing the sacred anthem
of faith and courage fought against
the tyrants wanting to enslave our folks.
Do please give ear to their laments.
O do you see their blood-stained tattered cloaks?

O mountain proudly bearing glorious history
Your legend rules the island's destiny.

Philippine Symbols

The mighty eagle lords the island's air.
The lowly carabao, the nation's working beast,
Anahaw's dark-green leaves, plant's luscious flair,
the ancient Narra tree looks to the east.
The flag with emblems bright: "Nation's not the least."
The sampaguita, Philippine jasmine –
 A spirit free is priceless like Ermine.

Monsoon Rains

August monsoon rains,
typhoons, strong steady winds, wet
soaky fields - farming.

Sailor, Beware

Seas that teem with creatures strange
sailors summoned– routes change.
Forms can trick you – looks are daunting,
fearsome, though some, stunning.
Formless voices heard beneath –
Quick: sword from its sheath!
Though bright horizons beckon you,
love awaits: be true.

Panaii

The golden stalks of rice in central plains
dance to the music of the wind
like gracious praise for God's abundant rains.

Gleaning harvest for their grains,
Panaiianons thank in gleeful jubilee
the golden stalks of rice in central plains.

The fields of Negros full of sugar canes
bear witness to its people's industry
like gracious praise for God's abundant rains.

The people of Panaii with willing strains
abide with planting season every year – the golden stalks
of rice in central plains.

Of the Almighty's boon for willing pains
Panaiianons sing with joy at harvest time –
like gracious praise for God's abundant rains.

The Harvest

Those golden stalks of rice in farmers' fields
are heavy now; it's almost time for yields.
The womenfolk prepare their threshing floors,
Their baskets stacked up high by their front doors.

"It's harvest time, oh yes, to fields we go!"
We sing with joy, "You harvest what you sow."
The women, all folks young and old – they dance
to celebrate the blessings of God's abundance.

Then offer they devotion to their God,
a fitting homage, thanks for their life's blood.
They dance and sing; they eat and drink to hearts'
content. They play so well each of their parts.

They hold a feast in honor of a saint
who helped them in their quest till faint.
With pomp and gaiety, with music free,
from morn till night, they feast in jubilee.

The Mardi Gras

The Mardi Gras is almost near!
It's held in January here
in honor of the Holy Child.
His Father to us reconciled.

May Flower Devotion

Ending May's traditional devotion
to the Blessed Maid,
singing from an ancient hymnal,
children's choral praises made.

Harvesttime

Harvest time is happy time.
oe'r the mounts of rice stalks climb
singing with their choice guitars
underneath the nightly stars.

On Courtship

Lads serenading maidens
under the shining moonlight.
Their voices are their tokens,
"My heart knows no flight!"

The favored lad still needs to show
sincerity through work to owe
the lady's family to see
as member-worthy he can be.

Jose Rizal and Love of Country

Jose Rizal, a friend and polyglot,
laid down his life for his beloved land.
To countrymen he was a patriot.
"To martyrdom your life had not been planned."

In Spain, you wrote your two great novels both
denouncing Spain's tyrannical rule oe'r
a once free people, now forced by an oath
to bow before the rule of rude colonial pow'r.

O noble soul, refresh our memory
of once a country with nobility
yet trampled on, insulted by an enemy.
for centuries without our liberty.

You woke us out of lethargy.
To fight for country is our sacred duty.

A Nation Lost

I once beheld a nation with great legacy.
Its seas teemed with species rare and shiny
declaring praises to His Majesty,
the Maker of it all. Yet man became too selfish.
He grabbed our pearls with wicked blunt relish;
we lost our pride, our sacred sovereignty,
our womenfolk, our solemn dignity.

For centuries, the "Pearl of Orient Seas"
shamelessly trampled by man's avarice.
Spanish guise of Christian faith, through
cross and sword conquered our spirits
until we rise Phoenix-like one day,
reclaim our land, our identity.
I lament our country's loss, our shared destiny
with heroes bold in the face of adversity.

Arise and Shine

Arise and shine, o favored in the land!
Heads always bowed in shame, saved by His hand,
His glory shines upon your radiant face.
Your story told by Peter's Little Band.

For once a slave but now you're free.
He walked with you as on the opened Sea.
The chains that shackled you he broke with pow'r;
the world at large your glorious freedom see.

Oh yes, how long we've waited for this day!
We risked it all, we dared - come what may.
With faith unwavering, we plodded on - and
now we're free! We sing, we dance, we pray.

Give thanks to Him who rescued you from them
who swallowed you in deathly bellies grim.
Yes, nation blest, my native Philippines,
so rare, indeed, is freedom's shining gem!

Your shining seas and plenteous verdant greens,
your seas with gleaming pearls make royal queens.
Your ancient trees, the forest is their home -
the inhumane cut down with every means.

O land with beauteous maidens God endowed,
of Malay race, though brown, you must be proud.
For precious freedom and your dignity,
great heroes died; to fight for you they vowed.

O Noble Rizal

O noble soul, your job is done -
our precious freedom for us won.
Your legacy imprinted bear;
in our hearts heroes' medals wear.

Your grace, with heroes brave, instill in hearts.
Your monument, your memory, never departs.
Among our brave and great forbears
you lie here witness to our flowing tears.

Yet, noble soul, you'll be saddened to see
the rich-poor rift as wide as Yellow Sea.
A people mixing their identity with greed
for wealth among the powers be.

O, great Rizal, please know my heart, truly -
awaken nation's sleeping loyalty.
O would that with sincere ascending pray'rs,
Heaven blesses nation's needful cares.

The Legend of the Barter of Panaii

"Sail on, sail on!" From tyrant king,
we fled for liberty.
Felicities we bring;
find here, we pray, our destiny.

We welcome you, o piteous ten,
Your wives, too, pray tell us –
what happened to you, men?
What fate will you discuss?

We come from Borneo, all ten.
We're chieftains in our land.
For weeks on sea tossed we have been
Till fate brought us on this white sand.

King Marikudo and his Queen
Maniwangtiwan smiling bold,
her garland necklace leaves of green
would trade for chain of gold.

The golden necklace is now hers,
the king a hat of shining gold.
The sale was done; an emblem bears
the contract for all to behold.

Panaii was thus to chieftains sold;
the natives to the mountains went.
All for gems and shining gold
the barter was a grand event.

They say this is the reason why
pygmies are found in the mountains -
the folks from islets of Panaii
gave way to ten Bornean chieftains.

Iloilo, Heart of the Philippines

My Iloilo, heart of country blest,
Your mountains grand, your trees that bend
with every changing wind - a faith, a quest
to be a light; our broken lives by Spirit mend.
To every neighbor, there's a hand to lend.
A quiet harmony borne out of tears
of Davids in our land that farmers tend.
Our people strong and sweet, our emblem bears
the sign of love – the Love of One who truly cares.

Mount Mayon

O lofty Mount Mayon, your perfect cone
is testimonial of God's wonderful
creation, now quiet yet watchful.
You sit kingly on your mighty throne
for deep beneath that cone is raging fire.
Reserved for times when, as in greedy Rome,
destruction fell on ancient Pompeii's dome.
Beware, you wicked, of Mount Mayon's ire!
For when the heart of man becomes corrupt,
the watchful eyes of gods are on the poor,
the lowly slaves, desiring nothing more
while greed desires Nature to disrupt.

But I am speaking of your elegance –
the world's most perfect cone - stunning radiance.

Life in the Village

Village fishermen go fishing in early dawn.
Taking up their trays,
the women start the threshing.
Grains are sifted from the chaff.

Cockfight is a game
famous in The Philippines.
Cocks are made to fight –
men bet – may the best cock win!
Gambling does take many forms.

Chinese game mah-jong
played by four on a table
Dotted dice and cubes
thrown here and there, determine
who goes home lucky tonight!

Tuba, local beer -
men drink to their hearts'
content. While to me, it smells,
Filipinos think it's sweet.
Drunk they go with tipsy steps.

Good Old Father "P"

There was an old and cheerful priest.
His priestly garb was a bit creased.
"Good morning, Father," once I said
soon as I rose from rect(o)ry bed.
His cheerful mien changed not the least.

"Today, I'm going home," he said.
"I will have breakfast there instead."
I thought his home was here upstairs
Where he is wont to say his pray'rs.
Out through the door, though, there he sped.

I learned that dear old Father "P"
had wife and children - four or three.
That's where he's headed for today;
I may not call - to my dismay!
He laughs with children running free.

That's dear old Father "P" – he's free.
He often goes out with such glee.
With family, he fondly roams
beneath cathedrals' grandiose domes.
Then sips his flavored English tea.

Once more, in the morning here he comes.
He holds the chalice with no qualms
It left me in a quandary -
I have it in his breviary -
Bathsheba's David, in the Psalms.

Philippines, Old and New

A country altogether old and new
comes bursting forth within the view.
Baroque cathedrals Spain inspired
with Moorish domes art had conspired.

Then in Manila, sprawling mega-malls
with hundreds of enticing Western stalls,
with food courts of international cuisine
a day's stroll through is like a labyrinth.

Deep in the mountains live Aborigines
with skin tone dark– of ancient origins.
Through seasons planting rice till they all fill
the fields at last – no more land left to till.

While in the cities, modern people thrive
on hamburgers and fries while streaming live -
"What's up with US politics and art?"
And bartenders keep pouring beer; they're smart!

The convent schools do still exist for those
who can afford to have their kids dispose
of money unworked-for, as though tomorrow
 never comes with unexpected sorrow.

Around the rural areas, farmers' kids
work hard while on the beach wealthy kids
are sipping costly drinks; they while away
precious time on needless holiday.

Rich mansions grace the city's pretty sights
of classic architecture on the sides.
With flowers rare their gardens bloom all year
for low-paid gardeners tend the buds dear.

Try going down beneath the bridges where
squalor, odious stench from everywhere,
alas, dismay the weary traveler.
A heap of trash, a little scavenger!

Stark contrasts like *the best of times and worst of times,*
thus Dickens' tale comes like a burst.
Society's comic irony -
by critic's scrutiny – a remedy?

Reflections of a Young Seaman

I am a Filipino
seaman, a lover of
the sea. I love the
gentle whispers of
the wind at night on
board the Seafarer.

But storms come –
as they come in life.
I hold fast to the pillar, the pillar
of my faith.
A knowing that a Hand
holds my hand, and I His.

Once we passed by the Straits
of Gibraltar – oh, what
marvels to behold!
Whales with glistening
backs, dolphins on the
shore, troops of rare birds
searching, hoping for a
place to hide in winter.

And me? Where am I heading?
One more night and the longing
for home will soon be over.

A Seaman's Soliloquy

Anchored on the shore of Nova Scotia,
our ship and crew at rest for days when,
while on a stroll I smelled the sampaguita,
the Philippine jasmine, whose fragrance
filled the air.

As if the ghost of bygone days came
back to haunt my lonely soul.
In a foreign land, I pause and
ponder – Who am I?

I am a Filipino seaman - young,
ambitious, bold. To seas I go – though
wont to stay – for poverty
beckons me to the open sea.
What future is for me there to behold?

God, help this poor man's soul.
Let not earthly quests blur
the vision of eternal shores.

Aurora, Hidden Philippine Paradise

Birds of the wild have found their habitation
in luscious forests of Aurora's land
where native tribes adhere to culture's brand;
"preserve our ways," their only supplication.
"Tradition, clan, old ways, our lasting stand.
On our ancestors' graves we vow to keep
communion with the rarest species of the deep."

Banaue Rice Terraces

Rice paddies on the steps of Mount
Banaue – ages hard to count.
The ancient tribes of Ifugows
carved hard round mountains with pained brows.
Their yearly yield is paramount.

In Baguio City, summer capital
of Philippines, these sights enthrall.
A Wonder of the World, these mounts
hold gems of luscious grains on mounds
of God's abundant earth for all.

Around the mountains tall, they grace
this Paradise on earth, o praise
man's ingenuity that knows
man's wisdom - it's to God he owes.
A wondrous city's banner, raise!

The Passion Play

Tradition's poem tells of Christ's most painful death.
Undying Love pronounced until His dying breath.
Most Christians of today, though, call it, "Good Friday."
 It was because on that same fateful, gloomy day,
a day of senseless, ruthless, Roman penalty,
The Christ forever changed man's awful destiny.
And that is why yearly, we do the "Passion Play"
with choral chants and hearts with sorrow on display.

But on the third day, angels moved the rock that sealed
His tomb. "O death, where is your sting?"[2] Love doesn't
    yield
to darkness but it always comes out in the light
to draw man from despair to hope's eternal fight.
The saving story did not end on Calvary –
He walks again on shore, the Man of Galilee!
He did not leave us orphans on this vale of tears;
He promised He'd be with us always through the years.

---

[2] *The New Testament Recovery Version.* 1 Cor. 15.55, Living Stream Ministry, 1991.

Easter

Lenten Season comes
- churches' altars full
Filipinos do
Jesus' death
Starting on Palm Sunday
forty days at which
Fridays are the days
Churches filled
contemplating
- dying on the cross
Easter culminates
Christ's resurrection,

with April showers
of purple flowers
commemorate
on Rome's Jewish state.
Lent does last
the faithful fast.
of fish - no meat.
with penitents who meet
Jesus' agony
for you and me.
the holy season:
our jubilation!

Christmas in the Philippines

The season starts at advent-tide
the poor, the rich, no more divide.
To church we go at break of day
with fragrant scents along the way.
The lanterns lit; the lights are bright.
For once, today the world seems right.

Then Christmas Day arrives and friends' pride laid aside
as the tree bends to celebrate the birth of Christ
and exchange gifts of love that's priced.
Let's go to church and greet the Child
of God – his heart is meek and mild.
A merry Christmas, one and all!
Glad tidings; do you hear Love's call?

On Immigration

Once I had the strangest dream -
among us was a gallant knight.
But we were boating on a stream
by Ellis Island on that night.

He said he found this bright new land
that seemed to be his destiny –
told how in England, his homeland,
he did not have his liberty.

I told a tale that's similar
From where I was, fairness, justice –
themes with which he was familiar –
came rarely as their winter solstice.

"Oh?" but he was not at all surprised.
I said, "I am from Philippine Islands."
"Moved to America?" he thus surmised.
He'd heard my lands were now Spanish lands.

I woke up from that dream and deeply thought
how many Filipinos here today
to this New World we have been brought
for precious freedom on the way.

America, our second home,
we hail your triumph over tyranny.
That like our heroes back at home,
you vanquished threats to sacred liberty.

We thank you for adopting us.
New sons and daughters share a destiny -
be white or black, yellow, brown, are thus
enjoying a new life in one fraternity.

Works Cited

Academy of American Poets. "Jose Garcia Villa." *Academy of American Poets*, www.poets.org.

Almario, Virgilio S. "Philippine Balagtasan (Verbal Joust)." *UCLA African Studies Center, 21* October 2003, www.international.ucla.edu.

Bradstreet, Anne. "Contemplations." *A Norton Anthology of American Literature*, edited by Robert S. Levine et al. 9th ed., vol. 1, W. W. Norton & Company, 2017, pp. 115-22.

British Empire. "Entering and Exiting the British Empire." *British Empire.CO.UK*, www.britishempire.co.uk.

Budiman, Abby, and Neil G. Ruiz. "Key Facts About Asian Americans, a Diverse and Growing Population," *Pew Research Center*, 29 April 2021, www.pewresearch.org.

California State University Bakersfield. "History of the Philippines." *California State University*, www.csub.edu.

Carbo, Nick, Editor. *Returning a Borrowed Tongue: An Anthology of Filipino and Filipino American Poetry*, Coffee House Press, 1995.

Damrosch, David, and Kevin H. Dettmar, editors. *The Longman Anthology of British Literature*, 4th ed., vol. 2C, Pearson, 2010.

Davis, Caitlin, and Jeanne Batalova. "Filipino Immigrants in the United States." *Migration Policy*, 8 August 2023, www.migrationpolicy.org.

de Ocampo, Esteban A. "Dr. Jose Rizal, Father of Filipino Nationalism." *Cambridge Core*, Cambridge UP, vol. 3, iss. 1, 24 August 2009, www.cambridge.org.

Department of Education. "Mapping Out Disadvantaged Groups in Education." *Department of Education.* 2007, www.files.eric.ed.gov.

Du Fu. "My Thatched Roof Is Ruined by the Autumn Wind." *The Norton Anthology of World Literature*, edited by Martin Puchner, et al., 3rd ed., vol. 1. W. W. Norton & Company, 2013, pp. 1318-9.

Du Fu. "Spring Prospect." *The Norton Anthology of World Literature*, edited by Martin Puchner, et al., 3rd ed. vol. 1, W. W. Norton & Company, 2013, pp. 131-8.

Embassy of the Philippines Madrid, Spain. "Malaga Mayor Gifts Philippine Embassy with Portrait of Spanish Explorer Ruy Lopez de Villalobos." *Embassy of the Philippines Madrid, Spain*, 15 February 2018, www.philembassymadrid.com.

Frost, Robert. "The Road Not Taken." *The Norton Anthology of American Literature.* edited by Robert S. Levine et al., 10th ed., vol. D. W. W. Norton & Company, 2022, p. 253.

Harvard. "The Treaty of Paris, The Religion and Public Life at Harvard Divinity School." *Harvard Divinity School*, www.rpl.hds.harard.edu.

Headland, Thomas N. "Agta Negritos of the Philippines." *Cultural Survival*, 17 February 2010, www.culturalsurvival.org.

Homer. *The Odyssey*. Translated by Robert Fagles, Penguin Classics, 1996.

Ileto, Reynaldo C. "The Unfinished Revolution in Philippine Political Discourse." *Southeast Asian Studies*, vol. 31, no. 1, June 1993, pp. 67-78, www.repository.kulib.kyoto-u.ac.jp.

Jacobs, Harriet. "A Perilous Passage in the Slave Girl's Life." *A Norton Anthology of American Literature*, edited by Robert S. Levine, et al., 9th ed., vol. 1, W. W. Norton & Company, 2017, pp. 886-9.

Jacobs, J. Bruce. "Whither Taiwanization? The Colonization, Democratization, and Taiwanization of Taiwan." *Japanese Journal of Political Science*, vol. 14, iss. 4. Cambridge UP, 30 October 2013, www.cambridge.org.

Joyce, James. *Dubliners. The Norton Anthology of World Literature*, edited by Martin Puchner et al., 3rd ed., vol. 2, W. W. Norton & Company, 2013, p. 1169.

Levine, Robert S., General Editor. "Slavery, Race, and the Making of American Literature." *The Norton Anthology of American Literature*, 9th ed., vol. 1, W. W. Norton & Company, 2022, pp 815-1066.

Levine, Robert S., General Editor. *The Norton Anthology of American Literature*, 10th ed., vol. D, W. W. Norton & Company, 2022.

Longfellow, Henry Wadsworth. Poems on Slavery. Excerpted from *The Complete Works of Henry Wadsworth Longfellow* 1902, 31 August 2023.

Longfellow, Henry Wadsworth. "The Slave Singing at Midnight." *A Norton Anthology of American Literature*, edited by Robert Levine S., 9th ed., vol. 1, New York, W. W. Norton & Company, 2017, pp. 709-10.

Macasero, Ryan. "Philippine Classroom Shortage Rises to 159,000 – DepEd." *Education in the Philippines*, 23 August 2023, www.rappler.com/nation/deped/-report-classroom-shortage-school.

National Archives. "Surrender of Japan (1945)." *National Archives*, www.archives.gov.

Poe, Edgar Allan. "The Poetic Principle." *The Norton Anthology of American Literature*, edited by Robert S. Levine, 10th ed., vol. B, 2022, pp. 653-4.

Poetry Foundation. "'A Psalm of Life' by Henry Wadsworth Longfellow." *Poetry Foundation*, www.poetryfoundation.org.

Power for Life Bible. Anthony H. Schuller, general editor, Faith Works, 2008.

Sanchez, Mark John. "The People Power Revolution, Philippines 1986." *Origin*. The Ohio State University, 22 February 202, www.origins.osu.edu.

Savella, Maria Theresa. "Languages – Mario Einaudi Center for International Studies - Cornell University." *Southeast Asia Programs*, www.einaudi.cornell.edu.

Shelley, Percy Bysshe. "Mont Blanc: Lines Written in the Vale of Chamouni." The *Longman Anthology of British Literature*, Damrosch, David, and Kevin H. Dettmar, editors. 5th ed., vol. 2C, Pearson, 2010, pp. 871-5.

Sholes, Owen D. "Bleeding Trees in the Poetry of Robert Frost." *The Robert Frost Review*, no. 26, 2016, www.jstor. org/stable/26476210.

Stanford University. "Immigration History." *Stanford University Medicine Geriatrics*, 2023, www.geriatrics.stanford.edu.

Stevens, Anne H. *Literary Theory and Criticism: An Introduction*, 2nd ed. Broadview Press, 2021.

Tagore, Rabindranath. *Gitanjali*. First Warbler Classics Edition, Macmillan and Co., 2021.

The National WWII Museum. "The Philippines Gained Independence from the United States." *The National WWII Museum New Orleans*, www.nationalww2museum. org. *The New Testament Recovery Version*. Living Stream Ministry, 1991.

USAID. "Economic Development and Governance." *United States Agency for International Development*, www.usaid.gov.

Wordsworth, William. "Lines Written a Few Miles from Tintern Abbey." *The Longman Anthology of British Literature*, Damrosch, David, and Kevin H. Dettmar, editors. 5th ed., vol. 2C, Pearson, 2010, pp. 429-33.

Wordsworth, William. "National Independence and Liberty," 17, *The Collected Poems of William Wordsworth*, Wordsworth Poetry Library, 1994, p. 377.

World Bank. "Philippines: Reducing Inequality Key to Becoming a Middle-Class Society Free of Poverty." *World Bank*, 24 November 2022, www.worldbank.org.

Yeats, William Butler. "A Prayer for My Daughter." *The Longman Anthology of British Literature*, Damrosch, David, and Kevin Dettmar, editors, 4th ed., vol. 2C, Pearson, 2010, pp. 2183- 5.

Yeats, William Butler. "Easter 1916." *The Longman Anthology of British Literature*, Damrosch, David, and Kevin H. Dettmar, editors, 4th ed., vol. 2C, Pearson, 2010, pp. 2181-3.

Yeats, William Butler. The Lake of Isle Innisfree." *The Longman Anthology of British Literature*, Damrosch, David, and Kevin H. Dettmar, editors, 4th ed., vol. 2C, Pearson, 2010, pp. 2177-8.